WATER AND LIFE

Barbara Taylor

Photographs by Peter Millard

FRANKLIN WATTS
New York • London • Sydney • Toronto

Design: Janet Watson

Science consultant: Dr Bryson Gore

Primary science adviser: Lillian Wright

Series editor: Debbie Fox

Editor: Roslin Mair

The author and publisher would like to thank the
following children for their participation in the
photography of this book: Terry Cook, Hussein
Hussein, Kyriako Kouvaras, Julie Lever, Freya Mehta,
Marlon Smith, Fayola Timberlake, and Umar Ullah.
We are also grateful to Julia Edwards, Evelyn
Mildiner, and Joy Mackey of Bounds Green Junior
School.

Illustrations: Linda Costello

© 1991 Franklin Watts

Franklin Watts Inc.
387 Park Avenue South
New York, NY 10016

Library of Congress Cataloging-in-Publication Data

Taylor, Barbara, 1954–
    Water and life/Barbara Taylor.
    p. cm. — (Science starters)
    Summary: Examines how essential water is to living
    things, both human and animal.
    ISBN 0–531–14116–0
    1. Water — Juvenile literature. 2. Biology —
    Juvenile literature.
    3. Aquatic biology — Juvenile literature. [1. Water.]
    I. Title. II. Series.
    QH90.16.T39   1991
    574.19'212 — dc20   90–32523
                                         CIP AC

Printed in Belgium

SAFETY
Always take care near ponds, rivers, lakes, or the sea.
The water may be cold, polluted, deep, or fast-
flowing and could be very dangerous. Make sure an
adult is nearby and look out for signs that warn of any
special dangers.

CONTENTS

This book is all about why plants and
animals need water, where water comes
from, and the effect of water on our
environment. It is divided into six
sections. Each has a different colored
triangle at the corner of the page. Use
these triangles to help you find the
different sections.

These red triangles at the corner of
the tinted panels show you where a step-
by-step investigation starts.

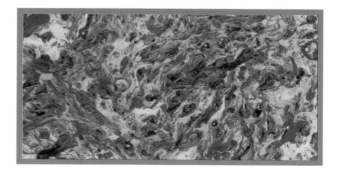

WATER FOR SURVIVAL

How many fish can you see on this coral reef?

Coral reefs are home to a huge variety of wildlife because there is plenty of food available. It was in the oceans that the earliest forms of life on Earth evolved thousands of millions of years ago. All life on Earth depends on water to stay alive. Without water, everything would die.

Water is the most important part of the bodies of plants and animals. They need water for all the chemical processes that keep them alive. Plants and animals that live in the sea, lakes, ponds, or rivers have water all around them, but animals that live on land have to drink water or get the water they need from their food.

Water helps to support a plant so it stays upright and keeps its shape. Like animals, plants are made up of tiny units called cells. When there is a lot of water inside cells, it pushes against the cell walls and fills out the shape of the plant. If you forget to water a houseplant, sooner or later it wilts, dries up and dies.

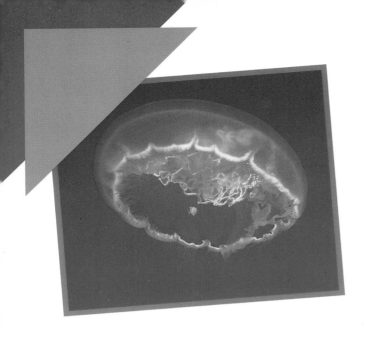

Have you ever seen a jellyfish washed up on the beach? A jellyfish is about 95 percent water. It has no shape at all out of the water and cannot survive. When a jellyfish is in water, its body fills out and takes on an umbrella shape. Muscles around the edge of the umbrella contract and expand to push the animal upward and sideways. When these muscles rest, the jellyfish slowly sinks down. Waves and currents in the water also help to move the jellyfish sideways.

The largest creatures in the world live in the sea. Water is about 800 times denser than air so it holds things up and supports them better. An animal as large as this humpback whale is too big and heavy to support itself on land.

One way to find out more about life in water is to carry out a pond survey. Draw a map of a pond and keep a careful record of the plants and animals that you find.

Remember to be careful near water. Sweep a net gently back and forth through the water and empty it into a dish. Look in different places, such as near the bank, among water weeds and in open water. Don't forget to put the plants and animals back in the water as soon as possible.

OURSELVES AND ANIMALS

Did you know that at least 60 percent of the human body is made up of water? Without water, you could not live for more than a few days. It is very important that all the different parts of your body contain the right amount of water. Your body takes care of this automatically, without you having to think about it.

Every day, you lose a lot of water when you sweat or go to the toilet. You also lose water each time you exhale. On a cold day, you can see a white cloud of water droplets hanging in the air when you breathe out. Another way to see this is to breathe hard onto a mirror. The mist on the mirror is the water in your breath.

Because you lose so much water each day, you have to drink a lot of water. You also take in a lot of water with your food. Some vegetables are almost all water. When your body needs more water, it tells you to drink by making you feel thirsty. You need about 2-2½ quarts or 8-10 cups of water each day.

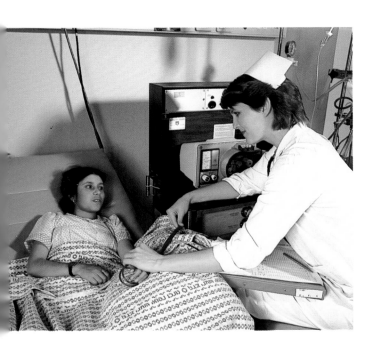

The kidneys control the amount of water in the body and clean the blood by removing poisonous waste products. About 160 quarts of blood are filtered by the kidneys each day. The waste products are then passed out of the body in urine. Most of the water and other substances needed by the body remain in the blood.

If a person's kidneys are not working properly, he or she may use a special machine that filters and cleans the blood.

MOVEMENT

When animals try to move through water, they are held back by the water pulling against their bodies. This effect is called drag.

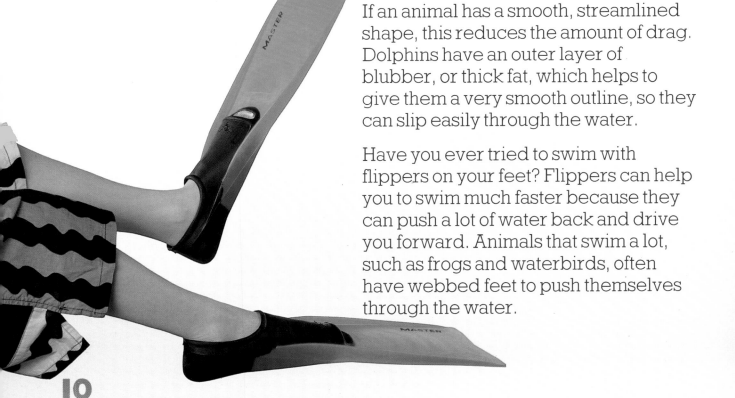

If an animal has a smooth, streamlined shape, this reduces the amount of drag. Dolphins have an outer layer of blubber, or thick fat, which helps to give them a very smooth outline, so they can slip easily through the water.

Have you ever tried to swim with flippers on your feet? Flippers can help you to swim much faster because they can push a lot of water back and drive you forward. Animals that swim a lot, such as frogs and waterbirds, often have webbed feet to push themselves through the water.

Many fish have a swim bladder inside their bodies. They can control the amount of air in the swim bladder to help them float higher or lower in the water. To find out how a swim bladder works, try this activity:

1 Use scissors to cut a sheet of thick, clear plastic into two identical shapes. You can make your fish any shape you like.

2 To join the two sides of the body together, cut some thin strips of plastic and glue them between the flat shapes. Leave a hole in the tail.

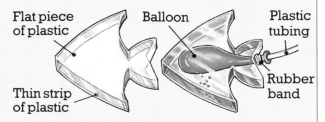

Flat piece of plastic

Balloon

Plastic tubing

Thin strip of plastic

Rubber band

3 Push a narrow plastic tube or straw into the neck of a balloon and keep the tube in place with a rubber band. Push the balloon inside the fish through the hole in the tail. Make sure there is a gap for the water to get inside the fish.

4 Put your fish into a tank of water and let it fill with water so it sinks to the bottom. Then blow air into your balloon swim bladder. The air will make the fish lighter so it rises up to the surface of the water.

PLANTS

Plants that live underwater do not need thick stems to support their bodies because the water holds them up. They usually have flimsy, feathery stems and leaves that will bend and sway with the current. The stems and leaves are often covered with a layer of slime to help prevent waterlogging. Most water plants have large air spaces inside their leaves to keep them floating in the water.

Water plants can take in water, dissolved gases, and nutrients over their whole surface. Land plants take in water through their roots and release it into the air through their leaves. The movement of water from the roots, up the stem, and out through the leaves is called the transpiration stream.

To see transpiration in action, tie a plastic bag around a shoot on a potted plant. Make sure there is a tight seal around the shoot. After a few hours, you should be able to see small drops of water inside the bag.

Over a large forest, such as this rainforest, the water given off by the trees may form a layer of mist and cloud. Rainforests have an important influence on the climate of the Earth. You can find out more about clouds on page 20.

How much water is there inside a plant? You could try weighing a fruit or vegetable, such as a banana, apple, carrot, or potato. Then dry it over a radiator (or ask an adult to dry it in an oven) and weigh it again. How much does it weigh after drying? In the pictures below, can you figure out which of the scales contains the dried banana?

To find out more about how plants absorb water, try this activity.

1 Half fill a container with water and add a few drops of food coloring or ink to the water.

2 Stand a leafy stalk of celery in the container.

3 After several hours, take the celery out of the water and slice off a thin section of the stem.

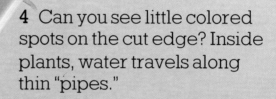

4 Can you see little colored spots on the cut edge? Inside plants, water travels along thin "pipes."

The stringy bits that sometimes get stuck between your teeth when you eat celery are these water pipes.

The spots you can see are the ends of the pipes.

5 Try cutting the stalk lengthwise. What do the pipes look like?

GROWING PLANTS

Many plants grow from seeds. A seed contains a developing plant and a supply of food. When conditions are right, the seed sprouts roots and shoots and starts to grow. This is called germination.

Do seeds need water before they can sprout? Put a layer of cotton balls into the bottom of two containers. Water the cotton in one container but leave the other one dry. Sprinkle some seeds onto the cotton balls in both containers and leave them in a warm place. What happens?

Which of these two containers has the wet cotton in the bottom?

We need water to grow crops for the food we eat. In some parts of the world, most of the year is hot and dry. Rain falls in just a few months of the year. The only way people can grow crops is to save water from the wet season so they can water or irrigate their fields when it is dry. Most irrigation systems involve a network of canals and ditches spread through the fields. More complex systems rely on sprinkling water over the top of the crop.

If too much water is taken from underground wells, or if no rain falls for several years, the land may turn into a desert. Then it is impossible to grow crops any more.

SOILS

Some soils, such as clay, are good at holding water. They can easily become waterlogged. In other soils, such as sandy soils, water runs straight through and is soon lost. Try pouring water onto different types of soil and measure the amount of water that drips through.

If there are plants growing in the soil, how does this affect the amount of water that passes through? The roots of plants help to hold water in the soil so it does not drain away so rapidly.

All over the world, people are cutting down forests and wild plants to make room for more farmland. But this land may soon be spoiled, if conditions are poor and the land is not well managed. Without plant roots to hold the soil together, water soon washes the soil away. And if the soil dries out, the wind may blow it away. This is called soil erosion. Farmers in some parts of the world plant hedges around their fields to try and reduce soil erosion.

In Madagascar, many of the forests have been cut down and soil erosion is a big problem. In this picture, the red gashes in the land show where the soil is badly eroded.

CLOUDS AND RAIN

Clouds are made of millions of tiny drops of water floating in the air. If the drops get too heavy to float in the air, they fall to the ground as rain. The rain collects in puddles, ponds, streams, rivers, and in the sea. When the Sun heats up this water, it turns into an invisible gas called water vapor. This process is called evaporation.

The water evaporating from a bowl of very hot water forms a small cloud of steam. This is because the invisible water vapor turns into liquid water as it meets the cooler air above the bowl. This is called condensation. The water vapor in the air around this cool drink has condensed to form drops of water on the sides of the glass.

The same thing happens high in the sky when water vapor meets cool air. It condenses to form drops of water which collect together to make clouds. The process of rain falling from clouds and the water evaporating and condensing to form clouds again is called the water cycle.

In places where there is a lot of rain, or where water cannot easily drain through the soil, swamps, bogs, or marshes may form. A common bog plant is sphagnum moss. The leaves of this moss have large empty spaces so it soaks up water like a sponge. Sphagnum is often used in hanging baskets to keep the other plants moist.

See if you can get some sphagnum from a florist or a garden center. Leave it to soak in some water. How much water can you squeeze out of the moss?

Philodendron plants grow in rainforests where it is very wet for most of the year. Their leaves are wide, thick, and glossy, with a waxy surface. This helps water to run off the leaf instead of soaking into it and making it moldy. The leaf also comes to a point called a drip tip, which lets water run off more easily. If water collects on the leaf, mosses may grow there. They make it hard for the leaf to live and grow properly.

DRY PLACES

In deserts, the small amount of rain that does fall comes in heavy downpours. The plants need to collect as much of this water as they can and store it for as long as possible.

Cacti are well adapted to survive in dry desert conditions. They have very long roots, which spread out in a network near the surface to collect rain. The stems of many cacti are pleated like a concertina so they can expand and store large amounts of water. Instead of leaves, cacti have sharp spines, which collect drops of dew in the early morning. The "wool" on some cacti may help to trap moisture near the plant.

High up on mountains, plants cannot easily take up water from the thin soils. Many of the plants grow in dense cushions, which trap heat and reduce water loss. Warm air can hold more moisture than cold air. The leaves of mountain plants may be hairy. The hairs help to trap valuable moisture. Some mountain plants can store water in their leaves.

THE SEASONS

In some parts of the world, such as central Africa, it is hot all the year. Rain falls only during a few months of the year, so there is a wet season and a dry season. In the dry season, in Tanzania, huge herds of wildebeest migrate vast distances across the grasslands to search for water and fresh grass to eat. They may move over 30 miles a day in order to find a drink. If water is available, wildebeest drink every day, but they can live for up to five days without any water.

In other parts of the world, the temperature changes throughout the year and there are four seasons – spring, summer, autumn, and winter. In autumn, trees with broad leaves shed their leaves. This is because a lot of water evaporates from the surface of these leaves and, during winter, the trees cannot get enough water from the soil to replace the water lost through their leaves. The fallen leaves rot down to form a rich compost that helps other plants to grow.

Trees with needlelike leaves usually have leaves all year. The thin shape of the needle and its waxy coating help to keep water from escaping. So the trees do not lose too much water through their leaves. The branches of many of these trees hang down so that snow can slide off them more easily, which helps to keep the branches from snapping.

POLLUTION

All living things need clean water to survive. But people have polluted much of the water on our planet with wastes from factories, farms, or homes. Factories may also make the water in rivers and lakes hotter, which means that the usual plants and animals cannot survive in it.

Rainwater can be polluted if poisonous gases from power stations and vehicle exhausts mix with water in the air. This makes the rainwater more acidic, so it is called acid rain. Acid rain makes building stone crumble away, harms or kills plants and animals, and makes the soil acidic. It also releases poisonous metals into the soil. Trees then absorb these poisons through their roots.

Trees with needlelike leaves are more affected by acid rain than broad-leaved trees. They lose a lot of their needles and whole forests may eventually die.

If oil pours into the sea when tankers clean out their tanks or if there is an accident, it can cause great harm to wildlife, such as sea otters. Oily fur sticks together and cannot keep out the cold and wet. The otters die if the oil is not cleaned off their fur.

To find out more about oil and water, try this activity.

1 Fill a bowl half full of water.

2 Put some drops of oil paint or marbling inks on to the water. (With oil paints, you will need to add mineral spirit to the water first.) Oil is "lighter," or less dense, than water and does not mix with water. So it floats in a layer on the surface. This is why an oil slick floats on the sea.

3 Use a fork or a straw to swirl the colors around until you have made a pattern that you like.

4 Gently lay a thick piece of paper flat on the surface of the water so that the paper takes up the color. Quickly lift it off again.

5 Hold the paper over the bowl to let the excess water drip into the bowl.

6 Leave the paper to dry.

This way of decorating paper is called marbling because the swirled patterns it produces are like the ones in polished marble.

MORE THINGS TO DO

Sorting out soils

Fill a large jar about one third full of garden soil and fill the rest of it up with water. Put the lid on the jar and shake it up well. Leave the soil to settle for a few hours. It will separate into layers of different sized particles.

Are the biggest particles at the top, bottom, or middle of the jar? Is the water clear or does it contain any soil particles? Can you see anything floating on the surface of the water? Repeat the same test with different kinds of soil.

Drinking water

Make a record of all the water and other drinks that you have each day. How much do you drink in a day or a week? If you have a pet at home or at school, see if you can find out how much it drinks in a day.

Evaporation test

Fill an egg-cup right to the brim with water and carefully empty this water into a saucer. Mark the level of the water with a pen. Now fill the egg-cup with water again. Leave the saucer and the egg-cup on a windowsill or a shelf indoors. What happens to the water levels after a day or so? Does the water evaporate faster from the saucer or the egg-cup?

Make a bottle garden

Find a large plastic bottle. Lay the bottle on its side and put some gravel and soil along the long side. Collect a few small mosses and ferns and press them carefully into the soil with some thin sticks. Make sure the soil is fairly damp. Put the lid on the bottle and leave your bottle garden to grow. It should not need any more water because the plants will give off water, which will condense to produce "rain" on the sides of the bottle. Your bottle is showing you a miniature version of the water cycle in action.

Drops of water

Gravel and soil

28

Air from plants

Cut a leafy shoot of Canadian pondweed and put it in a jar. All plants, including pondweed, give off a gas called oxygen when they make their food. They need sunlight to do this. If you put the jar of pondweed in some sunlight, bubbles of oxygen will soon appear. Time how many bubbles are given off in a minute. Then put the jar in a darker place, out of the sun. Does it give off any bubbles now?

Bubbles of oxygen

Pondweed

Test for acid rain

First you need to collect some rainwater. Pour the rainwater you collect into a clean, dry container and test it with indicator papers. The color of the paper will tell you how acidic the rainwater is. Rainwater is naturally slightly acidic, but if the water has been polluted by the gases from factories, power stations, or traffic, it will be much more acidic.

Test some lemon juice and some distilled water with the indicator papers. Lemon juice is very acidic and the distilled water is neutral. How does the acidity of the rainwater in your area compare with these other liquids?

Cloud shapes

Draw pictures or take photographs of the different types of clouds. Small, fluffy clouds that look like cotton are called cumulus clouds. They mean fine weather but may develop into huge, gray storm clouds. Clouds that are in long, thin layers are called stratus clouds. They bring rain or snow. Fine, wispy clouds high in the sky are called cirrus clouds. They are made of ice crystals and show that the weather is about to change and it may soon rain. See if you can predict the weather by looking carefully at the clouds in the sky.

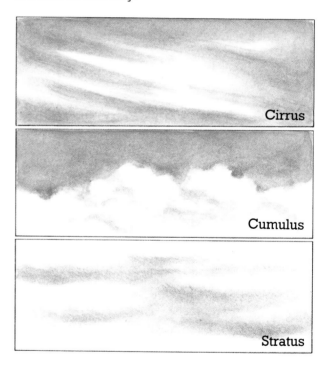

Cirrus

Cumulus

Stratus

Oil and water

Pour a small amount of water into a plastic bottle. Then carefully pour some oil on top of the water. It will float on top of the water in a separate layer. Now add a few drops of dish washing liquid, put the top on the bottle and shake it up. Is the oil still in a separate layer?

DID YOU KNOW ?

▲ Scientists think that the greenhouse effect will make the Earth's temperature rise by 3-7°F by the year 2030. This will cause flooding of low-lying areas and could lead to food shortages and other disasters. If the temperature rises by about 5°F, the Antarctic ice cap will start to melt and sea levels could rise by 16 feet or more. Antarctica is covered with a gigantic layer of thick ice weighing billions of tons. This ice cap contains more fresh water than all the world's rivers and lakes put together.

▲ A thirsty Arabian camel has been recorded as drinking 120 quarts of water at a time. The camel can live on this water for up to three weeks without drinking.

▲ Penguins have wings that are modified to form flippers. They can "fly" underwater at speeds of up to 25 miles per hour.

▲ It takes 10,000 pounds of water to grow 2½ pounds of rice. To grow 2½ pounds of wheat takes 1,000 pounds of water. Cotton needs much more water than these two food crops. 22,000 pounds of water are used to grow just 2½ pounds of cotton.

▲ The tiny duckweed plant floats on the surface of ponds and lakes. It is the smallest flowering plant in the world, measuring only one sixteenth of an inch in diameter.

▲ Cherrapunji, in northern India, receives an average of 430 inches of rainfall a year. In 1952, the island of Réunion, in the Indian Ocean, had 73 inches of rain in only 24 hours.

▲ The Blue whale is the largest animal that has ever lived on the Earth. It is over 98 feet long and weighs about 150 tons. This is about 30 times heavier than a male African elephant – the largest land animal.

▲ Sea turtles swallow seawater as they feed and much of their food is salty. To get rid of the extra salt, sea turtles secrete a salty fluid from special glands near the eyes. The fluid runs down their faces and, on land, the turtles look as if they are crying. Seabirds, such as gulls and penguins, produce salty tears for the same reason.

▲ The Water-holding frog of Australia lives in very dry places. When there is water available, it drinks as much as it can until it is very bloated. It produces a special outer skin layer to prevent water loss, and burrows into the soil. The frog can survive like this for many months, or even several years.

▲ The Kangaroo rat lives in the deserts of North America and never drinks. It gets some water from its food, but it also has several adaptations to avoid losing water. For instance, it has no sweat glands and produces very dry droppings. It stays in its burrow during the day and only comes out at night, when it is cooler.

▲ During a rainstorm, a Saguaro cactus can take up a ton or more of water.

▲ A Blue marlin fish has a perfectly streamlined body and can swim at least ten times faster than an Olympic swimming champion.

GLOSSARY

Acid rain
Rain that is much more acidic than normal because it has chemicals from vehicle exhausts, power stations, and factories dissolved in it. Acid rain can kill plants or animals or damage their growth. It can also cause damage to buildings and human health.

Cells
The basic building blocks of living things. Some living things are made up of one cell, others contain thousands or millions of cells. Most cells are so small that many thousands of them would fit on the head of a pin. The human body is made up of 50 trillion cells.

Condensation
The process by which a gas (such as water vapor) changes into a liquid (such as liquid water).

Density
The mass (weight) of a substance per unit of volume. Water has a density of 2.2 pounds per quart.

Dissolve
When a solid mixes completely with a liquid and does not settle.

Drag
The resistance to movement in water or air.

Evaporation
The process by which a liquid (such as liquid water) turns into a gas (such as water vapor).

Germination
The point when a seed starts to grow its first roots, shoot, and leaves.

Irrigation
Providing extra water for crops when rainfall is too low for their needs.

Pollution
The contamination of the environment with harmful substances.

Rainforest
Type of forest that grows on or near the Equator, where it is hot and wet for most of the year. Rainforests contain the greatest variety of wildlife on Earth.

Soil erosion
The process by which soil is blown away by the wind or washed away by the rain. It can be caused by cutting down trees, intensive farming, or poor methods of irrigation.

Streamlined
Something that has a smooth, slim shape which cuts through air or water easily.

Swim bladder
A gas-filled sac inside the body of bony fishes that helps them to change their position in the water by changing their density.

Transpiration
The evaporation of water through microscopic holes in plant leaves or stems. The transpiration stream is the movement of water from the roots up to the leaves of a plant.

Water vapor
The invisible gas that water turns into when it evaporates.

INDEX

Additional photographs:
Ardea 6(B); Alan Cork 19(B);
Chris Fairclough Colour Library
25(T), 25(B); Geo Science
Features Picture Library 26(T);
Frank Lane Picture Agency 26(B);
Peter Millard 10(T), 20(T);
Seaphot Limited: Planet Earth
Pictures 5(T), 24(B); Survival
Anglia 13(B); ZEFA 4, 6(T), 9(B),
17(T), 17(B), 19(T).
Picture researcher:
Sarah Ridley